MEMORY LANE
CREWE
Volume Three

MEMORY LANE CREWE
Volume Three

compiled by Gordon Davies

breedon books PUBLISHING

First published in Great Britain in 2002 by
The Breedon Books Publishing Company Limited
Breedon House, 3 The Parker Centre,
Derby, DE21 4SZ.

ISBN 1 85983 374 8

Printed and bound by Butler & Tanner, Frome, Somerset, England.

Cover printing by Lawrence-Allen Colour Printers, Weston-super-Mare,
Somerset, England.

Contents

Introduction

AS a journalist for more than 30 years I have always believed that there is one vital ingredient in every news story – people. We all enjoy hearing about people and, if there is one thing that beats reading about them, it is seeing them brought to life in pictures. That's why I have thoroughly enjoyed *Memory Lane Crewe Volume One* and *Volume Two*. They lived and breathed the modern history of Crewe in featuring hundreds of photographs of the people of the town as they used to say in the Mars Bar adverts, at work, rest and play. Gordon Davies' photographs succeed in telling the story of the town through its people. It worked with the first two volumes and it works again in *Memory Lane Crewe, Volume Three*. When we walk down Memory Lane it is not just the old buildings we want to see but the people on the street.

On the pages that follow you may well see yourself, somebody close to you, or people that you knew and even thought you had forgotten about. The memories came flooding back when I spotted the picture of former Crewe Alex goalkeeper Willie Mailey at a charity night. In an instant I was back there in the 1960s as a schoolboy worshipping every player who pulled on an Alex shirt. Mind you, players could really play in those days, not like today's highly paid fashion icons.

Well I remember, too, the *Ralph Reader Gang Show* at Crewe Odeon, the streamlined loco *City of Chester* steaming into Crewe and those wonderful days when every boy in the street was in the Scouts and looked forward for months to the annual camp.

That's the beauty of *Memory Lane Crewe, Volume Three*. Like the previous two volumes, there is something in it that is sure to delight everyone who lives in Crewe and all the members of that poorer breed of mortals, the Crewe exiles. Gordon's marvellous photographs open the door to a past that is still so tantilisingly close but of course, will never return. I, for one, am happy to go through that door and dwell a while and I am delighted that, in reading this, you are about to join me.

Dave Fox, Editor,
The Crewe Chronicle
2 High Street,
Crewe

Author's Acknowledgements

In compiling this book I have enjoyed the help of many people who have generously offered photographs or information which has supplemented my own archives. My thanks are extended to the following: Michael Bebbington, Margaret Mailey, Bill Bowden, Pam Graley, Jean Woodhall, Geoff Hillyard, Hazel Peake, David Williams, Mrs Aitkins, Mr Turner, Gareth Roberts, Doreen Hignett, Frank Ollier, Ron Barker, D. Richardson, Peter Wood, Roy Bradley, Peter Maddock, Dorothy Platt, Lance Vickers and J. Tibbetts.

I dedicate this book to
THE GOLDEN GIRLS
My sisters-in-law
ANNIE AND IVY

Crewe at Work, School and Play

Coronation Day celebrations in New Street in 1937.

A day to remember. Lockitt Street children and some of their mothers pose for a VE Day photograph on 8 May 1945.

With the arrival of the railways the population of Crewe has grown rapidly over the last 150 years, but not without a little help from the Maddock family. Peter Maddock, pictured here with his dog Archie, is a council worker of Middlewich Street, Crewe, and is currently tracing his family tree. He recently found this photograph which shows four generations of his family. His great, great grandfather, Harry Maddock, centre, was born in Manchester in 1854 and worked in the cotton trade before arriving in Crewe to begin an occupation in the shoe trade. He lived above his shop at 117 West Street.

Peters' great grandfather, John Maddock senior, left, was born in Ashton-under-Lymm in 1876. He left for Canada in 1893 and, after working as a farmer and a lumberjack, came back to England, joining his father in Crewe in 1893. He married Sara Alice Jones from No 9 Rigg Street and they settled down at 29 Richard Street. He took up occupation as a timekeeper in the Crewe Locomotive Works. Reginald Maddock, right, was Peter's grandfather. He was born at 29 Richard Street and worked all his life in the Crewe Works as a machinist, living at No 6 Broad Street when he retired.

Peter's father, John Maddock junior (centre), was born in 1924 at No 7 Sandon Street, where this photograph was taken. The street was demolished in the 1960s. He went to Ludford Street School before serving an apprenticeship in the Crewe Works. He lived at 169 Wistaston Road.

Since Harry first set foot in Crewe, the Maddock family now numbers more than 50.

This impressive building was Chester Place, Crewe, and was owned by the late Major H. P. M. Beams. Seemingly, he didn't like the Crosville busses passing along Chester Street in the 1930s. He would have been even more displeased if he knew that this fine looking building had been demolished and the Crosville Club had now been built on the land.

The old Wistaston Mill which stood empty and in a sad state of disrepair. It was modernised some years ago and is a house.

The wooden bridge spanning the Queen's Park lake, which was in place in time for the opening of the park on Saturday, 9 June 1888. The ceremony was performed by the Commander-in-Chief of the Cheshire Volunteers, Field Marshall HRH The Duke of Cambridge. The modern version of the bridge is of a more solid concrete structure.

The champion billiards team from the Broad Street Workingmen's Club in the 1950s.

Broad Street Workingmen's Club which opened in 1904 and closed its doors for the last time in 1997. There are now houses on the site.

Edward Mullen, pictured here in 1923, when he was driving the wagon of A. T. Latham, fruitiers, of Crewe.

This photograph was taken at the Creden Hill Camp, Hereford, when these four Crewe girls joined the RAF in 1961. They were later posted to the Hack Green secret nuclear bunker, Nantwich, where they worked together. Left to right are Glenys Yale, Norma Stockton, Gillian Chetta and Beryl Doody.

The Royal Scot train making its way up Shap in 1960. The Class 7 passenger engine pulling the heavy 13-coach train is 6223 *Princess Alice*, built at Crewe in 1937.

Streamlined engine No 6239 *The City of Cheste*r, pulling the Liverpool express, is seen here passing the Crewe coalyard on the down-line in 1939. Twenty –six of this *Princess Coronation* class were built, but five were not streamlined. Designed by Sir William Stanier, the first one rolled off the Crewe Works in 1937.

Fresh off the Crewe Works in 1933, engine 6200 *The Princess Royal* is waiting to haul the Euston to Carlisle express train after an engine change at Crewe Station.

A group of officials and two children outside the new Crewe North Junction signal box at its opening on 26 April 1958.

Crewe Locomotive Works employees from the Copper Shop, pictured during an away day in the 1950s.

A Crewe Locomotive Works first aid team showing off their haul of trophies in 1946. Also pictured are works management. This picture was taken outside the Works General Offices, a listed building which was destroyed by fire on Saturday, 23 July 1983.

The British Rail crew who took charge of the Royal Train for the investiture of the Prince of Wales at Caernarfon on 1 July 1969. Tommy Hope (second from the left) was the train driver. The guard that day was B. Campion, far right of picture. Tommy, a friend of the author, died in July 2002.

Other local British Rail staff who were involved with the preparation of the Royal Train for the Prince of Wales's investiture on 1 July 1969.

A line-up of apprentices and staff at Crewe Locomotive Works Training School in 1955.

Crewe Works erecting shop staff on a day out at Matlock in 1956.

Tender Shop workers from Crewe Loco Works line up for a photograph before leaving for their annual fishing match in 1957.

Crewe railway station porters caught on a 'photo break' on platform six in 1949.

Inter-City railway staff receiving their good service awards from area manager Jan Glasscock in 1986. Left to right are Joe Kettle (guard), Freddie McQuade (guard), Jan Glasscock (area manager), Eric Heatley (driver), Nigel Cadman (driver) and Robert Charlesworth (chargeman).

Crewe fireman Bob Longworth after receiving his long service award in 1992.

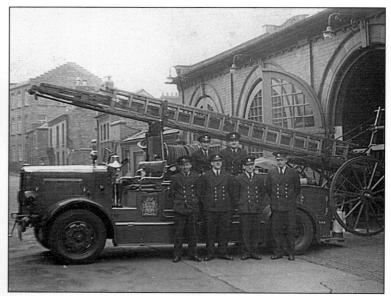

Crewe firemen with an appliance of the day, when the fire station was in Beech Street in 1961. In the background is the old Beech Street School which was demolished to make way for the new Market Centre. The new £84,000 County Fire Station opened on Crewe Road on 18 July 1966. The firemen pictured are (back row left to right) Bill Taylor, Marsh Cartwright. Front row: Jack Harding, Sam Caruth, Johnny Norman and Colin Tyrell.

A Christmas party at the old Beech Street Fire Station in 1964.

Home Office, Minister of State, Miss Alice Bacon, inspecting the a parade of firemen at the opening of the new station in Crewe Road on 18 July 1966.

Gathered around the fireman's pole with firefighter, Colin Tyrell at a mid-1960s Christmas party.

On parade at the opening of the new fire station on 18 July 1966.

Crewe firemen in a charity fire engine pull in aid of the Springfield Special School in 1984.

Fireman Gareth Roberts, with a couple of youngsters on board his fire engine at a flag day on the Crewe Market Square in 1980.

Christmas time at the Camm Street CWS clothing factory in 1961. Among those pictured are Christine Foden, Mrs N. Foden, Hazel Stamps, Hazel Peake and B. Walton.

A trip to Blackpool for these members of the Broad Street Workingmen's Club in 1933.

Crewe CWS machinists pictured outside the Camm Street factory on 26 May 1949. Left to right are Sheila Yoxall, Margery Bennet, Betty Robbins, Dorothy Lewis, Milly Jones, Madge Cocks and Hazel Hayes. The CWS factory is now a leisure centre.

In September 1955 Smethurst & Holden shirt factory staff on Queen's Street enjoyed a trip to Blackpool to see the illuminations.

Girls from the CWS clothing factory in party mood at the Pioneer Anglers Club in 1962.

Pretty young Crewe chemists' assistants pose for the camera before a 1961 party.

The Duke of Westminster with Mornflake Oats staff during a visit to the factory in 1970.

Boy drovers at the Crewe (Middle) Cattle Market in 1943. Left to right are Mr Tom Farrell, Vincent Wakeley, Jack Morris and Gordon Davies.

Mr Earnest Wright, managing director of Henry Manley and Sons, pictured on market day at the Crewe Cattle Market in the early 1970s. This area now forms part of Crewe Alexandra's huge car park.

Kendall and Sons Ltd of 72 Market Street, Crewe, advertising useful Christmas presents in 1910. The window display is made up of umbrellas, walking sticks and mirrors.

The Barker Street Cattle Market shortly after its completion in 1951 to replace the corrugated iron construction which had stood since the early 1900s. The entrance land foyer to the Barker Street site would have done any cinema proud. It also housed a luxurious restaurant and offices with a sales ring, shippons and loading bays. The market was officially opened by the Earl of Shrewsbury in January 1951. The Barker Street site was demolished in 2001 and was the last of Crewe's three cattle markets. The area is now covered by housing.

A gathering of officials and guests who attended the opening luncheon of the Barker Street Market in 1951.

A Crewe Market stall holder for 40 years, Mr Frank Wood is seen here receiving his prize from the Mayoress of Crewe after winning the Market Coronation competition in 1953. Looking on is the Mayor of Crewe, Councillor Frank Roberts, and Mr Wood's wife, Elsie.

Jim Butt pictured after winning a St John Ambulance individual trophy in the early 1960s.

A Crewe Locomotive First Aid team pictured with the works managers in the 1950s.

Young Punch and Judy man Alec Jones.

Some members of the South Cheshire Frets Orchestra which was founded in 1989 by Brian Jacklin, initially as a vehicle to enable his music students to experience 'ensemble playing'. Since then the orchestra has grown from ten players to its current 25 musicians. Since its formation the orchestra has made three foreign tours, in 1991 visiting Sofia in Bulgaria and in 1993 appearing at the American Mandolin Convention in Nashville. In 1998 the orchestra visited Sousse in Tunisia for the international music festival. The members on this photograph, which was taken in 1990, include (back row, left to right) Teddy Scholfield, Gareth Richardson, Judy Phillips, Marian Cheshire and Alison Maxwell. The two girls front middle are Nicky Phillips, left, and Alexandra Richardson. Brian Jacklin is in the foreground.

Crewe County Grammar School Old Students' Association Amateur Operatic Society – 'Old Studs' – dancers at rehearsals for *The Dancing Years* at the old Crewe Grammar School in 1964.

Dancers pose for a picture during the 'Old Studs' production on *Kiss Me Kate* in 1965.

Rehearsals for the 'Old Studs' production of *Gipsy Love* in 1966.

The cast of the 'Old Studs' production of *The Dubarry* in 1970.

Pupils who took part in an Adelaide Street School play in 1950. Not all of the names are known, but included on the picture are Teacher Mr Kearton and pupils John Blount, Derek Johnson, David Williams, Roy Birtles, Cyril Bennion, Valerie Bennion and Carol Bennett.

Young dancers from the Yvonne School of Dancing, pictured during rehearsals in 1985.

Gemma Robertson and Josh Williams were the youngest pupils at The Yvonne School of Dancing in 1985.

Youngsters pose around the Christmas tree at their school nativity play in the 1980s.

Bedford Street School pictured before demolition in 2001. The school has now been replaced by housing.

A group of youngsters fancy dress in the 1960s.

These children from Broad Street and Vere Street look a bit bemused as they wait to board a bus for a trip to the seaside in 1964, thanks to the kindness of Mrs M. Moore, (second from the right of picture). Mrs Moore owned the corner shop in John Street and ran an annual trip for the children of the area.

A girls' choir of 1954.

It is the summer of 1956 and this is the last class of 4T2. Back row (left to right) are T. Steadman, D. Farnell, J. Perry (teacher), M. Butt and B. Cooper. Middle row: D. Lancaster, L. Jones, C. Ray, T. Holt and R. Tomkinson. Front row: J. Bryant and B. Burgess.

Broad Street School pupils and teachers posing for a school photograph in June 1952.

A Borough Senior School netball team pictured in 1940. Miss Vickers was the teacher while the only other names known are Doreen Dutton, Hazel Hayes and Barbara Leighton.

A photograph that will rekindle memories of schooldays. In 1990, Victoria High School staff pose with school leavers.

Elaine Bebbington and her entourage smile for the camera at the Underwood West Infants School's Queen's Silver Jubilee celebrations in 1977.

Pupils and staff at the Underwood West Infants School in 1980.

Pupils from the Coppenhall High Comprehensive School on an Outward Bound course to Barry Island from 19-26 April 1980.

Guest stars at a Crewe charity evening in 1966. Left to right are Willey Mailey (Crewe Alexandra), actress Betty Alberge (*Coronation Street's* Florrie Lindley) John Mahoney (Crewe Alexandra), Yvonne Ormes (Miss Nantwich), not known, and young singer Cathy Jones, who also appeared in *Coronation Street*.

From one local girl to another. Yvonne Ormes,(right), winner of the Miss United Kingdom title, presenting Carolyn Moore, with the Miss Rhyl trophy in 1970. Carolyn went on to win the Miss Great Britain title later in the 1970s.

Former *Coronation Street* star, the late Bill Waddington, (Percy Sugden) pictured with his admirers when he made a personal appearance at a local charity shop in the 1980s.

A happy Yvonne Ormes is welcomed home by neighbours, young and old, after winning the Miss Great Britain title in 1970. Proud father Ken is pictured on the extreme left.

Tracey Mullineux (right) being congratulated by the previous year's winner, Tracey Winwood, after winning the 1991 Miss Crewe and Nantwich title.

Nine-year-old Jacqueline Pritchard with her dog Smudge, when she was one of the finalists in the Miss RSPCA competition in 1969.

Shavington Rose Queen, Kim O'Reilly, with her assistants.

A line up of models at a 1955 Dorothy Perkins charity fashion show at Crewe Corn Exchange. The Corn Exchange was demolished in the 1970s to make was for the extension of the Municipal Buildings.

The late Jimmy Williams, centre, pictured when he first opened his cycle shop in Mill Street in 1946. On the left is George Henshall and on the right, Ron Mellor.

Jimmy Williams outside his cycle shop in 1950. All the shops have since been demolished, and the area, in Mill Street, has been landscaped.

The Crewe Branch of the National Association of Cycle Traders, pictured at meeting on Wednesday, 18 August 1954.

Cyclist Jackie White, taking part in a time trial race in the early 1980s.

Councillor Ray Stafford (left) and Cyril Grocott assisting David Williams to 'postcode' cycles on the Crewe Market Square in the 1980s.

Posing in 1984, on Crewe Market Square, before a cycle 'Fun Run', this group of smiling cyclists look ready for the open road.

Cyclists, left to right, are Brian Lewis, Geoff Hillyard and Gordon Davies, pictured in Wales, on the edge of Lake Bala in 1948.

Welcoming two young sailors from the ship HMS *Ambuscade*, who had just arrived after a charity cycle ride in aid of the Holmelea Children's home – which used to stand in Macon Way – are the Mayor and Mayoress of Crewe and Nantwich Borough, Mr Charles and Mrs Dorothy Hassall in 1980. HMS *Ambuscade* was decommissioned that year.

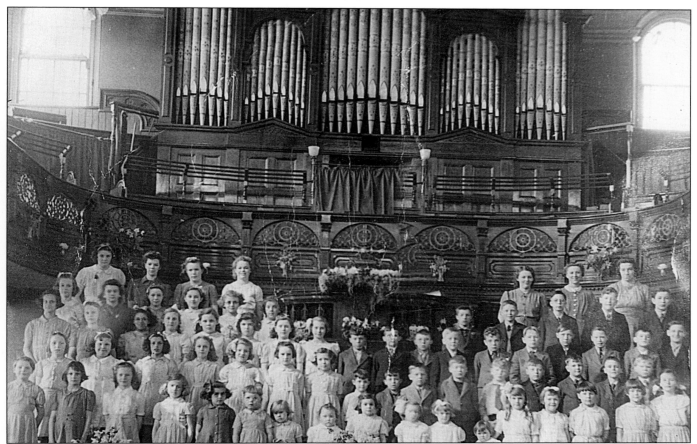

Crewe Trinity Methodist Church Sunday School anniversary photograph taken in 1943.

A social gathering at North Street in the 1980s. The Revd Tagg is pictured in the centre of the group.

The 1985 Winter League winner, Brian Yearsley, receiving his trophy from Crewe Golf Club captain, Don Tomkinson.

Karate girl Julie Ollier, pictured in the 1970s.

Crewe Golf Club Winter League winner, Alan Foster, receiving his trophy 1980.

Crewe Golf Club captain, Colin Yoxall, 1983.

Roy Griffin curling 130lbs in the 1960s.

'Ossie' Wright at the snooker table in the 1960s.

Mick Osbourne in action on the baize on 27 December 1968.

Norman and Betty Vaughan, licensees of the Broughton Arms, Haslington, welcoming, Mr C. Bithell (right) and Mr D. Round during a 'Meet the people' campaign in the 1970s.

Pools winners Mr and Mrs R. A. Armstrong, receiving their cheque for £38,059.50 on 20 May 1989.

Angela Hassall with a Hearing Dog For The Deaf.

Susan Crossley and kennel assistant, Kathryn Sylvester pictured with their trophy and rosettes after a Crufts win in the 1980s.

John Wright (left) and Mark Brookshaw with the Scanner Appeal salver in 1992.

Gulf Support Group veterans pictured at the dedication of a commemorative stone in Crewe's Queen's Park on 28 July 1991.

It was 'Rabbits, Rabbits, Rabbits' for Dianne Stubbs and Rachel Hopley as they took part in an Easter Bunny competition.

Train driver Garvice Upton with two young passengers at Stapeley Water Gardens.

Teddy Scholfield and Tony Hayes in harmony at the Bridgemere Gardens in 1980s.

Clarinetist David Jefferies proudly displaying his Royal School of Music award in 1989.

Winning musician Jeff Sparkes, showing off his trophy after a win in 1990.

Harry Foster with his trophy and prize-winning bloom in 1984.

Willaston 'bobby', Tom Lawton, receiving a tankard from the villagers on his retirement in 1975.

Crewe wrestler Count Bartelli (Geoff Condliffe) presenting his annual sporting award to Mark John Gray in 1986. Looking on is writer Ann McRory.

Carole Stockton with her pony in 1976.

Princess Anne meeting locals during a visit in the 1970s.

Kitchen staff at Hungerford Road School in 1980. Pictured are Margaret Mailey, Doreen Carvell, Sheila Carlin, Pearl Moss, Wendy Johns, Edna Swift, Lynn Edwards, Vera Simpson, Margaret Nevitt, Margaret Stubbs, Audrey Davies, Margaret Bowers and Jackie Neild.

The Crewe Vagrants ladies hockey team, 1995. Back row (left to right): Janet Wells, Janet Freeman, Sheridan Tomkinson, Tracey Ticehurst, Beryl Griffiths, Helen Lanson. Front row: Sue Myers, Donna Brown, Rachel Hill and Tracey Chew.

Councillor, John Bedson unveiling a plaque at the Crewe Heritage Centre in 1990, watched by the Mayor and Mayoress of Crewe and Nantwich, Councillor and Mrs Alan Pheasey. The name of the other person is not known.

SALVATION ARMY

Salvation Army members shortly after the opening of the Citadel in 1889.

This photograph was taken on 17 August 1907 and is believed to be of the first Crewe Salvation Army band. Included on the photograph are Bandmaster William Garrett, on double bass is Roger Dutton (a former mayor of Crewe), Tom Dutton, George Buckley, Harry Bebbington, George Pettitt and Fred Jones.

Young Salvation Army members with their officers in 1928.

Cadet Bandsmen with officers in 1928.

A Salvation Army Christmas party for senior citizens in 1938, sees Crewe Borough Mayor, Councillor Harry Bricker, left of picture, trying his hand at 'waiting on'. Mr Bricker was the licencee at The Earle of Crewe public house on Nantwich Road, Crewe.

Salvation Army members pose for a photograph before boarding their bus to go on duty in the 1950s.

A pageant at the Salvation Army headquarters in Market Terrace in the 1950s. Included on the pictured are F. Dickinson, H. Bebbington, E. Newton, S. Smith, J. Cattell, S. Bebbington, S. Wadkins, T. Singer, L. Dean, A. Harrop, Mrs Rowles, J. Cattell, Adj Thompson, Mrs Thompson, Mrs Singer, J. Peers, G. Dean, E. Bailey, W. Cattell, Mrs Davies, L. Davies, Elsie Parsons, Mrs Watkins, Mrs Bailey and H. Buckley.

Crewe Salvation Army songsters in the 1950s. Back row (left to right): H. Lightfoot, T. Dean, B. Wray, A. Goodson, A. Becket, A. Bobs, T. Jones, C. Newton, N. Singer, T. Newton. Middle row: E. Peers, D. Heywood, unknown, A. Harrop, C. Newton, Mrs Tunney, K. Newton, R. Jewkes, Mrs Hall. Front row: M. Lightfoot, H. Buckley, unknown, E. Brooks, G. Smith, K. Bobs, M. Goddard, M. Mailey, R. Wray, Captain Reid, O. Beckett, Mrs Captain Reid, E. Edmonson, S. Newton and L. Griffiths.

Crewe Citadel band in the 1960s. Front row (left to right): N. Edwards, J. Cottell, L. Brooks, T. Heywood, H. Beckett. Middle row: Captain L. Beadle, C. Newton, G. Singer, E. Peers, P. Sheplar, C. Griffiths, S. Smith, K. Dean, unknown, Dean, E.Kitter, Mrs Captain Beadle. Front row: C. Lightfoot, B. Wray, C. Newton, R. Griffiths, E. Cain, T. Dean, T. Haywood, G. Dean, T. Newton.

The new Salvation Army Citadel taking shape in Prince Albert Street in 1960. It replaced the old building which was built in 1889 on Market Terrace, now Queensway.

Market Terrace – now Queensway – as it was in 1960, with Marks and Spencer on the right. Next is the old Salvation Army Citadel, while further along is the rear entrance to Woolworths. To the extreme left of the photograph is the old Co-operative jewellers shop, which is now Ottakers bookshop.

The old Salvation Army Citadel being demolished in 1961.

Crewe Borough Mayor, Councillor Don Holt, welcoming an international and Crewe group of Salvation Army members to the Municipal Buildings in 1973. Councillor Holt was the last Mayor of the old Crewe Borough and was chairman of the district until it became the Borough of Crewe and Nantwich in 1974.

SCOUTS

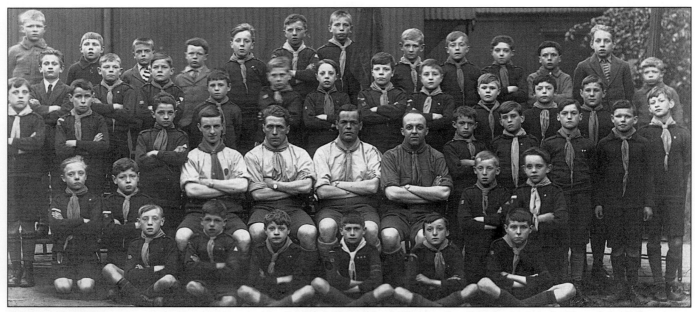

A St Andrew's Scout troop in the 1920s outside the 'Tin Church', which was the first St Andrew's Church building.

Geoff Vernon and Joe Shaw with young Scouts enjoying a 'nosh up' at a summer camp in 1937.

Scoutmaster W. H. (Jimmy) Cooke, centre front, with the St Andrew's Scouts at a 1932 summer camp.

A 1930s male and female Scout troop.

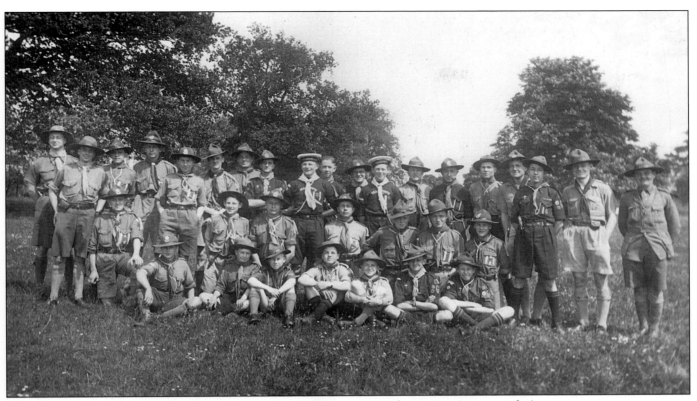

St Andrew's Scouts in their Sunday best at a 1937 summer camp with two Sea Scouts as their guests.

A wartime photograph outside the Convent building – now the police training centre – in Salisbury Avenue (note the brick wall in front of the windows to prevent bomb blast damage). Major Nixon is making a presentation to one of the Scouts. Doris Muckley is to Major Nixon's right, while Joe Shaw is further along the line, in Scouts uniform.

At Kibble Stone camp in 1947.

19th South-West Cheshire Scouts at camp at Brynbach in 1945.

A troop of 1947 with the Revd Wilson in the centre of this photograph taken in the garden of the new St Andrew's Church.

The 1st South-West Cheshire Cubs and Scouts pictured on stage during their troop show *Crackers* in 1948.

Yet more fresh faces in this post-war group taken in the grounds of the new church building.

Hungry mouths waiting to be fed at a Whitsuntide camp in 1950.

Outside the Crewe Odeon in 1952, before watching *The Ralph Reader Show*.

An Easter Camp at Barthomley in 1952.

St Andrew's Scouts visiting the Battle of the Flowers festival on the island of Jersey in 1953.

The St Andrew's Scouts group around a floral 'Cheshire Cat' during their visit to the Battle of the Flowers festival on Jersey in 1958.

It was a very large cast for the Gang Show *Joyride* staged in 1953. Here they are seen at rehearsals at a local chapel.

A St Andrew's Scouts anniversary in 1956. This large group made the birthday cake look very small. I hope there was enough to go around.

A Group Scout committee in 1956.

Not much to sing about! This camp fire group look thoroughly wet and miserable as they struggle to keep warm while at summer camp at Falmouth in 1962.

The Mayor of the old Borough of Crewe, the late Councillor Sidney Bayman, meeting the St Andrew's Cubs during a visit in 1971.

A group of 'Ancient' Scouts at the 1966 St Andrew's troop's 50th anniversary celebrations.

A 1971 Scout group.

The Ugly Sisters and the Woodchoppers in the Scouts' 1971 pantomime *Cinderella*.

The Lord Derby Shield, which was first competed for in 1923, was won by a team from St Andrew's Scouts in 1976. Included on the picture are Venturers C. Jones (captain), N. Lowe, A. Ward and D. Weston and Scouts A. Cliffe (captain), J. Nasse, S. Pearson, A. McGarrigle and I. Cliffe.

The chorus line from *Cinderella* in 1971.

The late John 'Pimmer' Partridge, left, receiving the Scouts' Associations Silver Award from County Commissioner Derek Oliver in 1985. Looking on is County Commissioner Ray Salisbury.

A 1976 1st South-West Cheshire group celebrating the 60th anniversary of the St Andrew's troop. Included on the picture are former Scouts, present Scout members and guests.

The 1st South-West Cheshire Scouts Reunion of 'Ancients' pictured at the Scout HQ in Bedford Street when the troop celebrated its 80th anniversary in 1996. Back row (left to right) are Dave Hollowood, not known, Peter Manning, John Manning, Philip Broadhurst, Peter Garnett, Brian Moss, Ian Broadhurst, Mick Malpass, Bill Jones, Stuart Ashman, Arthur Siddons, Dennis Beswick, Tony Thompson. Middle row: Ray Davenport, Peter Roberts, Harry Williams, Ken Dickens, Tony Billington, Gerald Blagg, not known, Albert Siddons, Mike Bennion and Howard Flood. Front row: Malcolm Kelly, Ian Broadhurst, not known, John Gresty, Fred Jones, Ron Barker, Roy Bradley, Alf Clewes, Aubrey Brazier and John Campion.

A group photograph taken after the 1976 church parade to mark the 60th anniversary of the St Andrew's Scouts.

ATHLETICS

Ann Johnson, a Crewe sprinter who ran at Wembley in the 1960s.

Susan Markert.

S. Pidock.

Marathon runner Syd Hope.

Physiotherapist Mick Gill with a trio of Crewe marathon runners.

Graham Flood.

Johnny Kettle.

Ian Farrington.

Suzanne McCall.

Pat Haines.

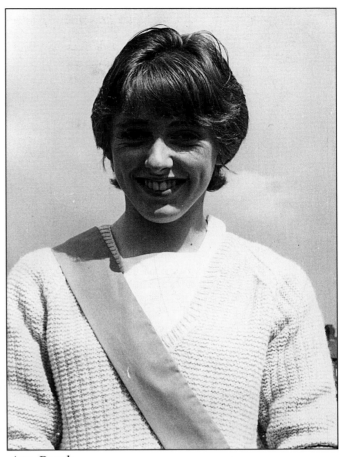

Ann Booth.

Caroline Shakeshaft.

Duncan Stone.

Timothy Birtles.

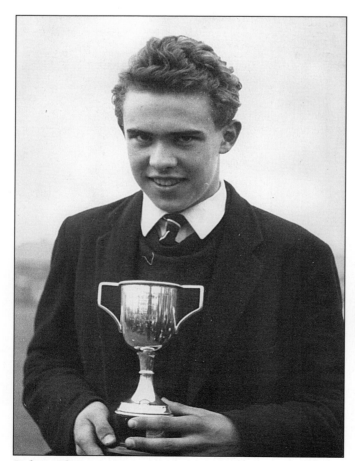

Robert Blaney.

Trevor Smith.

TENNIS

Competitors at a South Cheshire tennis tournament on 13 July 1957.

It's all smiles for the camera as the successful competitors receive their trophies at a 1962 tournament. Urban District Council Chairman, Rowland Bowen, presented the prizes.

Competitors leaving the court at a Nantwich tennis tournament on 21 May 1960.

A group of tennis league officials and prize winners at an annual presentation evening on 23 October 1962.

Prize winners and officials at the tennis championships on 6 June 1964.

Tennis league officials and players with their trophies at a social evening on 7 November 1964.

Methodists in league tennis in the early 1960s.

Cheshire Dairy Queen, Miss Ann Thompson, who presented the trophies, is pictured with her ladies-in-waiting, officials and prize winner at the Nantwich and South Cheshire open lawn tennis tournament at Barony Courts, Nantwich. Pictured are R. W. Stone, H. B. Clare, Miss Sadie Piggott, G. R. Smith, F. L. Vaughan, Miss Thompson, Jack Maybury (referee), Mrs Stones, Miss Mary Jackson and Mrs Smith.

A group of tennis prizewinners at the Earle of Crewe Hotel on 26 November 1966.

BADMINTON

Dr and Mrs Turner pictured with a group of winners at the Nantwich and Crewe Badminton Finals in the 1950s.

The Hospital Street Methodist team, champions of the Crewe Badminton League in the 1950s. Pictured are (back row, left to right): J. Sproston, G. Bull (captain), L. Williamson, and E. C. Sutton. At the front are Miss D. Thomas, Mrs P. Sutton, Mrs R. Young and Miss G. Young.

Badminton player Janet Grice pictured in 1969.

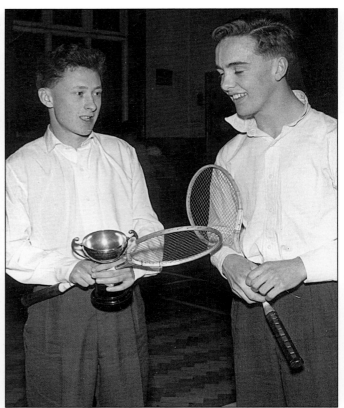

Sixteen-year-old Alan Jervis (left) with Derek Penlington after winning the Crewe and District Badminton League tournament in 1956. Alan went on to win 30 league titles in the next 30 years.

Successful badminton players with their trophies at a Crewe League tournament in 1970. Left to right are Brian Tandy, Margaret Jervis, Alan Jervis, Aileen Holland, Alan Oakes, Ella Haighton and Helen Fowles.

Badminton League president Jack Maybury presenting the prizes at a tournament on 19 October 1967.

Miss Suzanne Pace receiving her cup from Badminton League chairman Geoff Bull, after winning the Stan Smith Memorial Trophy on 1 April 1961.

Former Manchester City player Glyn Pardoe presenting ladies singles winner Aileen Holland with the Crewe and District Badminton League trophy, watched by runner-up Ella Haighton in 1970.

Players who took part in the Crewe and District Badminton League's Robert Leyland Tournament in the 1970s. Pictured are Mike Ashton, Mark Watts, Jack McCaigue, Mike Pumford, Steve Holmes, Paul Golds, Yvonne Govey, Michelle Duncar, Val Griffiths and Alison Bowker.

DARTS AND DOMINOES

Anthony Morris, who won a heat of the Carlsberg Darts Tournament whilst on holiday at the Blue Water Holiday Village, Seaton, on 20 October 1982.

Mick Clowes 1964.

Tommy Gregory.

Brian Lewis.

Hughie Leitch, pictured after winning the Club Union Darts knockout trophy.

Frank Edge.

Peter Frazer.

Reg Malcolm.

Tom Smith, who used the same set of arrows for 15 years.

Bill Morgan.

Jeff Price.

Fred Palin.

Dave Randell.

Harold Sharpes.

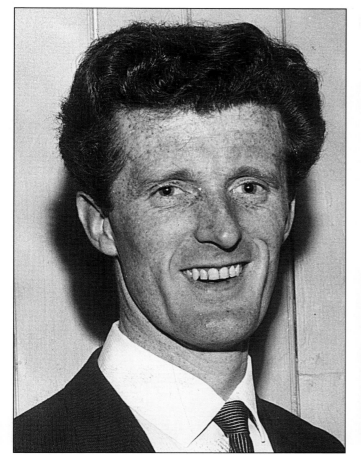

Malcolm Swinney.

Eric Heath.

Harry Everett.

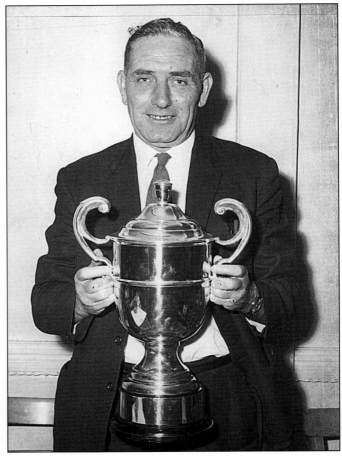

Tom Povers.

Fred Palin.

John Winstanley.

Rex Wilkinson.

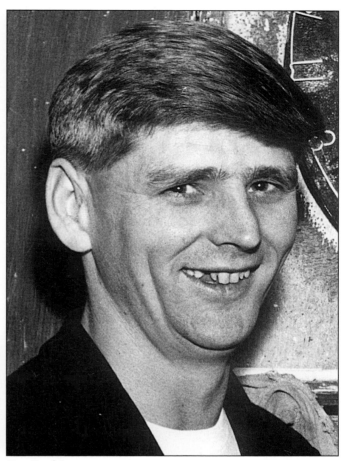

Ray Probin.

Bill Caldicott.

Harry Cooper.

Les Gallimore.

Bill Owen.

George Snowdon.

Bill Hart.

Jim Meyler.

Ernie Challoner.

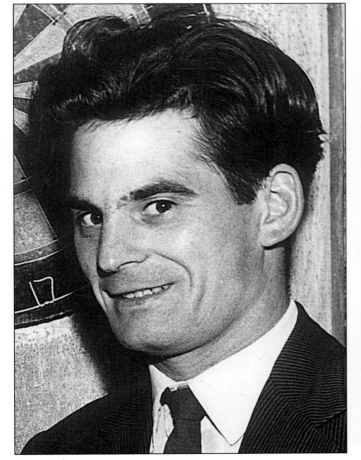

Brom Clowes.

George Cooper.

Walter Fleet.

Geoff Allott.

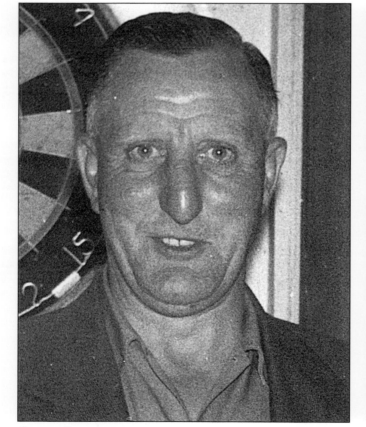

George Scane.

Dick Heaton.

Albert Davies.

Joe Bostock.

Roy Bickerton.

Arthur Hughes.

Frank Huxley.

Bill Mellor.

Walter Fleet.

Dave Clarke.

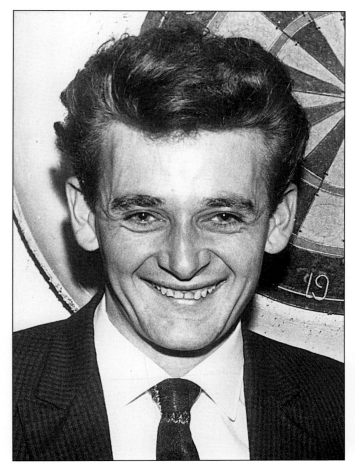

Trevor Howells.

Bill Westbrook.

Les Jones.

Sydney Goodyear.

John Platt.

Derek Brandreth.

John Griffin.

Ron Heaton.

Peter Boughey.

Herbert Davenport.

Miss B. Patrick.

Kath Probin.

Toni Boyer.

Mrs Foxley who was Crewe's oldest darts player in 1961.

Mabel Cowling.

Nellie Dowling.

Kath Tomlinson.

Eddie Hill.

Ron Catterall.

Arthur Farrell.

Arthur Hughes and George Scane after their win in the Club Union Finals.

Rolls-Royce 'A' darts team, May 1964.

The Rifleman 'A' team on 16 February 1963.

The Spring Tavern darts team, 17 November 1962.

Darts pair, brothers Alec (left) and Dennis Allcock who played for the Vine at Shavington in 1964.

The Egerton Arms darts team, October 1962.

Captains of the Crewe Club Union darts teams with their trophies at the presentation evening at the Coppenhall Club.

Darts pairing Fred Everall (left) and John Roberts in 1964.

A 1964 Chronicle darts pairing, Les Forster (left) and Bob Bryan from the Holly Bush.

Charlie Conde (left) and Alex Bradeley who paired up in the Crewe Chronicle darts competition in 1964.

The Rifleman 'A' darts team who took part in the Crosville darts competition on 12 October 1963.

The Rifleman 'A' team after winning the Licensed Houses League trophy in 1964.

1960s darts pairs champions Rex Wilkinson (left) and Tom Wilkinson.

Ladies darts trophy night at the Liberal Club in the early 1980s.

The Lord Nelson darts team pictured on 2 March 1963.

A Rifleman 'A' darts team of the 1960s.

The Raven darts team on 23 March 1963.

Darts pairing Matt McAllister (left) and Brian Nolan.

Reg Gerrard.

Local darts players who raised £200 for the Homeleigh School in 1984.

Stan Gerrard

John Challinor.

Frank Addis.

Trophy winners at the Crewe and District Ladies Darts Premier League presentation evening at Coppenhall Working Men's Club on 13 December 1984.

Mother and daughter darts pairing in the Chronicle Charity Darts Competition in the 1960s were Mrs F. Benningwood (left), and Mrs M. Howells.

Crewe Alexandra goalkeeper Willey Mailey presenting the Licensed Houses League Supreme Darts Championship Cup to captain Dennis Dawson and his team in the 1960s.

Norman Woolley.

Brian Timmis.

Bob Thomas.

The Vine, winners of the LVA Darts League in 1963.

Denis Reade after winning the Club Union KO trophy in the 1960s.

Freddie Brookes.

Alf Dale who took part in the 1963 Chronicle Darts knockout competition.

Ind Coope League champions Belle Vue 'A', after winning the domino league on 22 September 1962.

Ron Imber, who qualified for the News of The World championship in the 1960s.

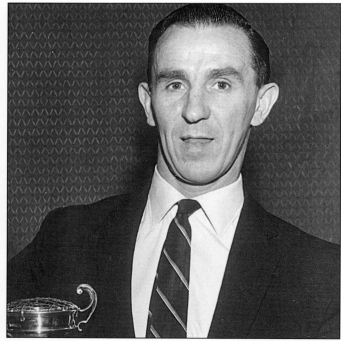

David McPherson of The Bridge, Madeley, pictured with his trophy after winning the individual Merit Championship Dominoes Cup in the Wrinehill and District League in 1963.

BOXING

LMR boxer Derek Hampton, who was employed as a fitter in the Crewe Locomotive Works.

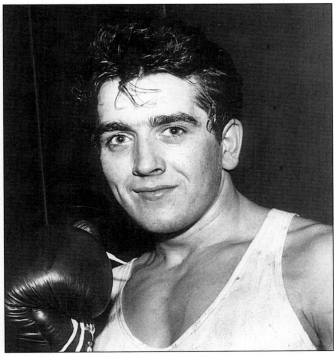

Tom Fraser, who boxed in the 1960s.

Youngster Malcolm Worthington receiving a trophy after yet another win.

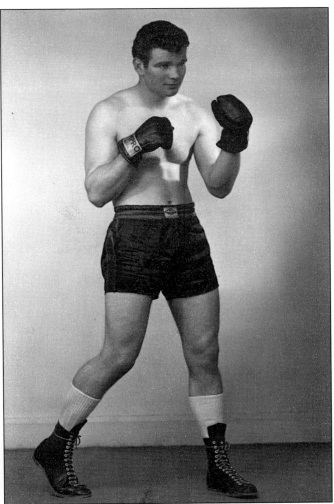

An early photograph of Malcolm Worthington.

Jim Cunningham in 1961.

An award taking place in the boxing ring on 28 April 1956.
Pictured are F. Benion (left) and Stan Dutton.

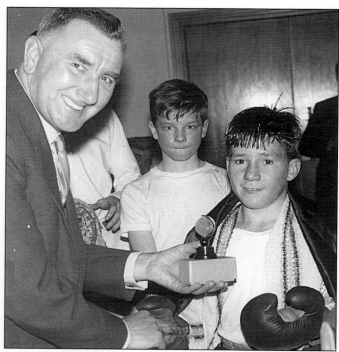

F. Fitzgerald receives his trophy from Stan Dutton in the
1960s.

Colin Chesters who had won five out of eight fights when
this photograph was taken on 13 March 1954.

Crewe LMR heavyweight Athol Ewington in 1962.

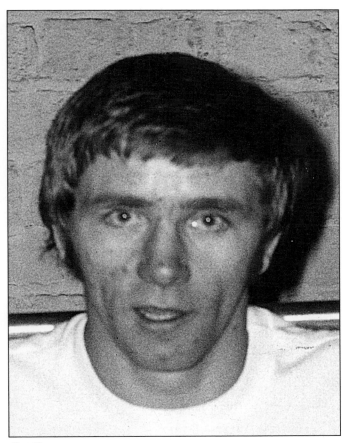

Pat Brogan.

Schoolboy boxer Michael Oliver.

Mark Atkins.

Karl Kerin.

Dave Elliott.

Boxer Jim Cunningham (left) and a colleague at work in the foundry in the Crewe Locomotive Works in 1961.

Tony Smith.

Alan Welch.

HOMING

It's the South-West Cheshire Homing Federation annual general meeting and prize distribution evening on 31 January 1959 and former Crewe Alexandra footballer George Price (second from right) receives his prize after clocking a winning bird.

The Three Pigeons Homing Society members ringing their birds for a race on 27 April 1961.

White Horse pigeon fanciers pose for a picture on their awards night on 11 November 1961.

South-West Cheshire Homing Federation at their awards evening on 25 January 1958.

Nantwich Premier Flying Club members at their end-of-season dinner and prize presentation on 5 December 1957. Mr Roberts, who presented the prizes, is seated third from left. On his left is the club president, Mr Boffey.

Wilf Hart is certainly a man who has a winning way with birds. At least he did in Jubilee year, 1977, when he was one of the district's most successful pigeon fanciers. That year, Wilf, who is now 64, was the envy of fellow members of the Crewe West End Flying Club where he scooped the Old Bird Combined Averages Cup, Channel Averages Cup, Angouleme Trophy, the Tom Manley Memorial Trophy for both old and young bird races, the Jack Brown Trophy and the Longest Channel Race Trophy. He also took first place in the club's Gloucester open race and his bird was first home in Cheshire in the National Flying Club open young bird race from Avranches in which 10,115 birds took part.

As if that wasn't enough, he entered the West End Club's Christmas show taking first prize and special prize with the same bird while another of his entries took a fourth place. Wilf started racing on his own account in 1971 after being in partnership with his late father, William Hart. By the end of 1977, Wilf had won £1,395.

Wilf is pictured with an impressive array of just a few of his many trophies.

Faddiley pigeon fanciers at their presentation evening on 28 December 1957.

Mr John Jackson presenting the Combined Average Trophy at the White Horse Flying Club dinner on 28 November 1964.

Faddiley Pigeon Club at their annual dinner and awards evening on 2 December 1967.

Wrenbury Fanciers at their awards evening on 27 February 1960.

Mrs Speed presenting the Wrenbury Homing Society awards on 22 December 1962.

The Premier Flying Club dinner and awards evening on 13 December 1958.

Wrenbery Homing Society dinner and prize presentation, where Mrs Speed presented the trophies on 14 December 1963.

Mr John Jackson presenting the Jackson Shield at the Premier Flying Club on 19 December 1964.

Premier Flying Club members with their awards on 7 December 1963.

SWIMMING

Cynthia Hawkes with her swimming trophy in the 1960s.

Marilyn Surridge.

Elizabeth Cordery.

Bill Ryder.

Susan Lowe.

A happy group of Crewe Swimming Club members with their haul of trophies.

Swimming Club chairman Mr G. M. Harvey presenting the members' gift to secretary, Mrs J. E. Smith in appreciation of her recent work, at a Christmas party in December 1954.

Newly-elected Crewe Swimming Club officials on 10 March 1966.

Neil and Lynette Brooks.

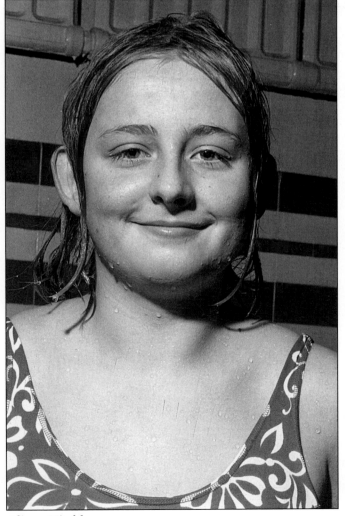

Alison Hitchbon.

Stephen Webb.

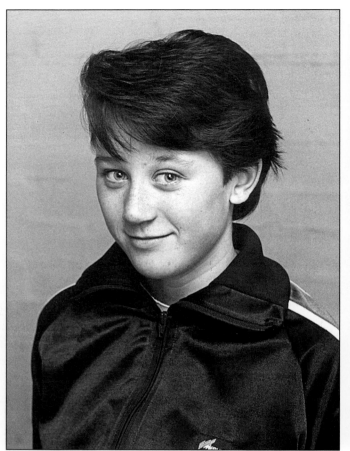

Caroline Walton.

David Chesters.

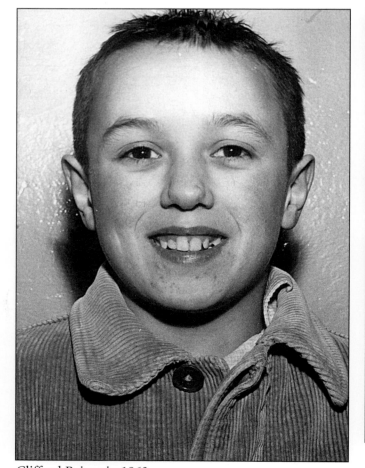

Clifford Baines in 1963.

Dot Wolfenden with her swimming awards in the early 1980s.

TABLE TENNIS

Lou and Audrey Moran.

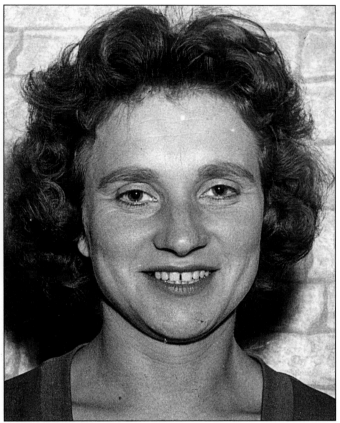

Eileen Edwards.

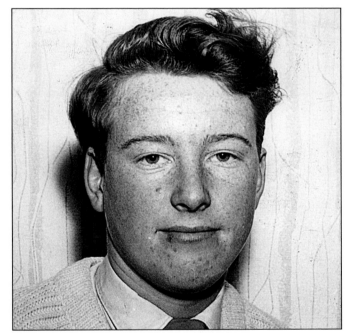

Alan Waddington.

J. Roddan, pictured on 3 March 1967.

T. Lovatt, 3 March 1967.

Ray Nicholls.

Irene Robbins.

Roman Lewandowski.

Tony Greene.

Terry Turner.

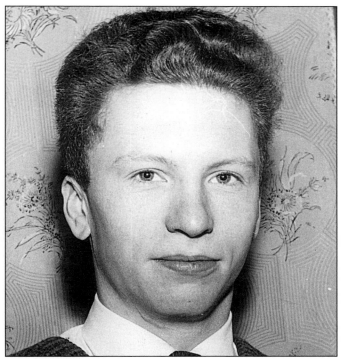

Barry Whittle in the 1960s.

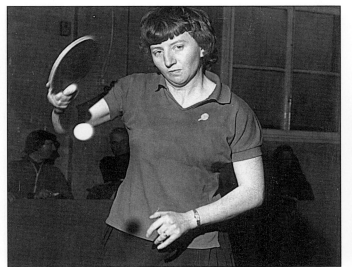

Sylvia Upton.

David Bunting.

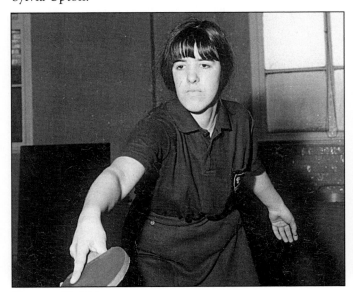

Sharron Halliday.

Ann Jones, 3 March 1967.

Stan Morgan.

Tony Morgan, 13 March 1969.

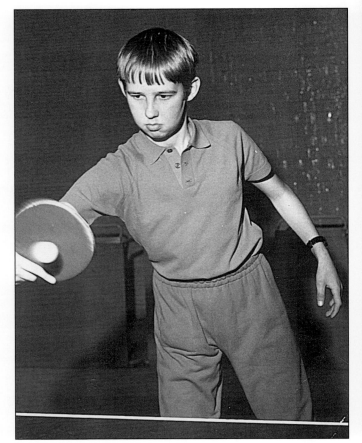

Paul Steele.

Lou Moran.

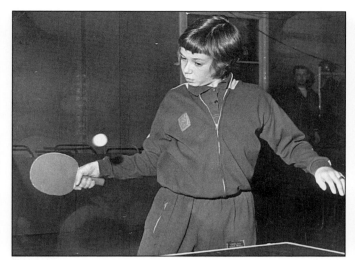

Trevor Burrows.

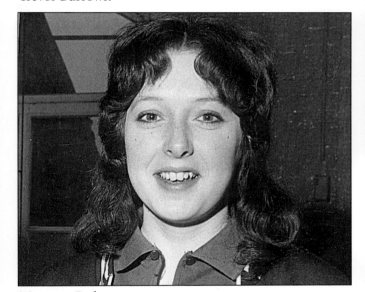

Margaret Bedson.

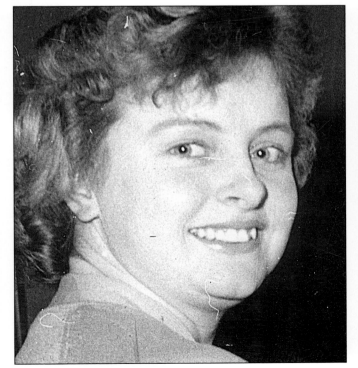

Pat Collier.

John Hignett.

Ken Steele.

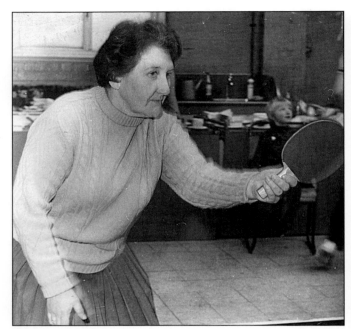

Mrs Irene Robbins, who was a table tennis singles winner at 50 years of age.

Carol Tew.

Ray Platt, a table tennis singles champion of the 1960s.

Young Sherie Boomla in action at the Goddard Street railway canteen in the 1970s.

David Jackson serving at the old LMR Canteen in Goddard Street.

Neil Smith.

Steve Taylor.

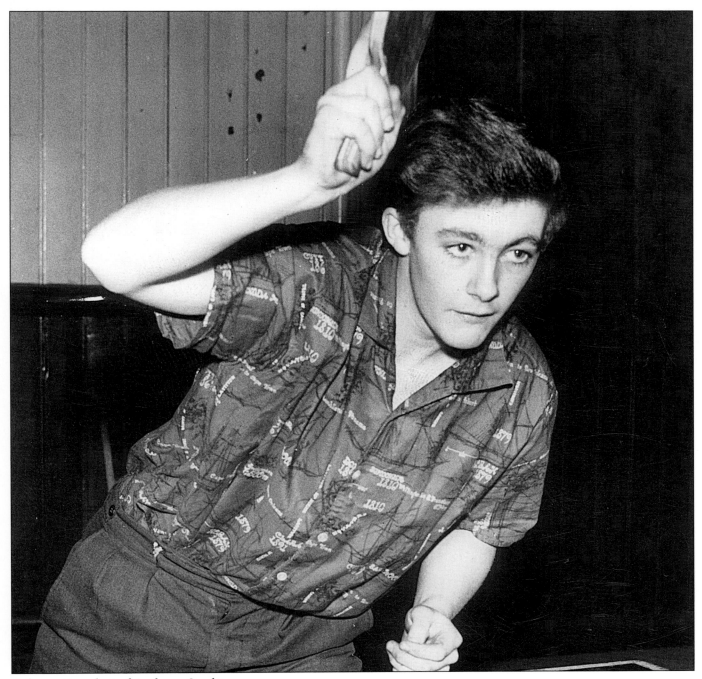

A fine action shot of Anthony Stockton.

MOTOR SPORT

Ralph Raffles (left) and Guy Harvey pictured with their three-litre Jaguar car in which they took part in the Dutch International car rally in April 1951.

Some of the men who steered the Motor Club to the top, pictured on 17 December 1966.

Some of the competitors who took part in the Night Owl Rally on 12 September 1959 take time out for some last-minute map plotting.

Motor Club members and guests at a social evening on 6 April 1957.

Motor Club chairman Reg Walley (centre) presenting 'thank you' gifts to club stalwarts Jack Thomas (left) and Percy Taylor at the club dinner on 28 January 1956.

Five Motor Club members who between them had given more than 150 years' service on 8 February 1964. Left to right are V. Cooper, V. Walley, P. Taylor, J. Thomas and J. Harrison.

A Motor Club presentation evening in the 1960s.

Vernon Cooper preparing his car for the Swedish Rally on 14 June 1958.

H. Richard, L. H. Hickson, R. T. Burton and Vernon Cooper preparing to take part in the annual Cheshire Rally on 19 March 1960.

Veteran works rider Bill Doran, a guest at the 1955 Motor Club dinner, takes to the saddle on Bill Webster's TT-winning Velocette, encouraged by (left to right) Phil Carter, who won the trophy for the best 1954 club member, Bill Webster, who captained the winning club teams at the Isle of Man TT and Leinster, and Wilf Billington, a member of the victorious Leinster team.

Peter Jackson and Allan Pilbury with their safety rally trophies on 9 May 1964.

Geoffrey Vernon.

John Bebbington was Motor Club member of the year, 20 February 1965.

Motorcycle scrambling at Bowsey Wood on 13 October 1967.

John Done scrambling at Hatherton in October 1969.

Chris Horsfield competing in a scramble on 6 April 1967.

Bill Webster receiving a gift from Mrs Vernon Cooper for outstanding achievement in motorcycle sport on 6 February 1960.

Scramble rider Brian Nadin pictured on 11 April 1964.

Thrills in the Hatherton mud on 25 November 1966.

John Done poses for a picture at the Hatherton track on 11 April 1964.

Scrambler Alan Clough, 10 March 1962.

Chris Whittle, Moto-Cross schoolboy champion, on 26 February 1981.

Bob Trotter.

Charlie Scarboro, a reserve for Crewe Kings who rode only once for Crewe, at Long Eaton in 1971. He remained at Crewe and ran a training school in the mid 1970s.

Australian Paul O'Neil, who rode for the Crewe Kings speedway team in 1969-70.

New Zealander Colin Tucker rode for Crewe Kings in the 1969-70 season.

Warren Hawkins, who rode for Crewe Kings in 1970.

Crewe Kings rider, Rob Jackson, in the 1969-70 season.

Glyn Blackburn appeared for Crewe Kings in the 1969-70 season.

Geoff Ambrose, who rode for Crewe Kings from 1973 until 1975. From 1973 until the mid-1980s, he also owned a motorcycle business opposite the Earle Street track.

CRICKET

Machine Shop South staff pictured at a presentation at the Western Sports Club after winning the Crewe Works Cricket KO competition in 1952.

Elworth Cricket Club.

Aero Aces, a Rolls-Royce cricket team, 1970s.

Another Elworth cricket team.

Haslington CC team.

A Rolls-Royce team.

A Crewe CC XI, 1980.

A Crewe CC team, 1990s.

A 1980s Crewe CC team.

Crewe CC team, 1980s.

Elworth CC.

A Rolls-Royce cricket XI, 1980s.

A Crewe cricket XI, 1990s.

Crewe LMR cricketer H. Simpson.

Neil O'Brian.

Alan Janninson.

Khushid Armad, the LMR professional in 1964.

Australian all-rounder Lou Laza was the LMR professional player and coach.

Nantwich CC pictured on 23 June 1955.

Another 1980s Rolls-Royce XI.

Len Muncer of Crewe LMR CC, 1955.

Rolls-Royce CC, 1980s.

Winners pictured at a Crewe CC awards evening.

Rolls-Royce player, J. Prince.

Rolls-Royce batsman, Gordon Walker.

Tony Betts.

LMR cricket captain Chris Marks.

LMR cricketer Dennis Armitage.

A former LMR CC captain, the late Jeff Clarke.

Brian Hough, 1960s.

Selby Bailey.

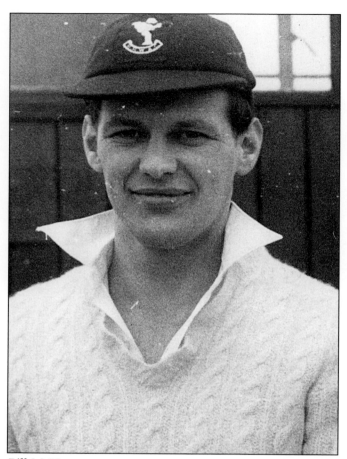

Bill McHenry.

Dick Collins.

Bill Bailey, who played for Rolls-Royce and later with the Nantwich CC.

Tony Cooke.

Jimmy Clayton.

Howard Simpson.

Gerald Hardstaff.

Fred Goodwin.

Stuart Wood.

Ernie Pointon.

Eric Barnes.

The late Eric Keeley, for many years a fast bowler with the Rolls-Royce CC.

Fred Procter.

John Morris.

Gordon Harris.

Leonard Blunt, 1949.

The Crewe CC junior team in 1962 when they won the Kidsgrove Junior Cricket League.

Captain Stuart McLeod (centre, front row) with his Rolls-Royce team of the 1980s.

Elworth CC hamming it up for the camera, 1980s.

Lancashire and England Test batsman Cyril Washbrook signing autographs for young fans during a visit in the 1950s.

Len Morris, a former Crewe CC professional.

A Crewe LMR cricket team of the 1950s.

A Crewe CC team pictured at the Vagrants' ground in the late 1970s.

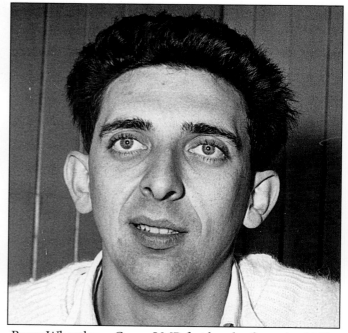

Barry Wheatley, a Crewe LMR fast bowler from the 1960s.

A Permanent Way cricket team of the early 1980s. Back row (left to right) are Chris Highfield, Peter Hopkins, David Crillion, Steve Addis, John Vickers, Dave Cooper (professional) and Roger Mason. Front row: John Cooper, Livingstone Critchlow, Dave Williams (captain), Alan Bailey and Jeff Harding. The mascot is Andy Williams, son of the captain.

A Permanent Way cricket team from 1960.

John Waters of LMR CC.

Eric Stubbs, a fast bowler who played with Crewe LMR before joining Nantwich CC in the 1970s.

LMR cricketer, the late Tony Latham.

LMR cricketer Alan Mumford.

Roger Febery.

Bob Davies.

Former LMR cricketer Ray Shallcross.

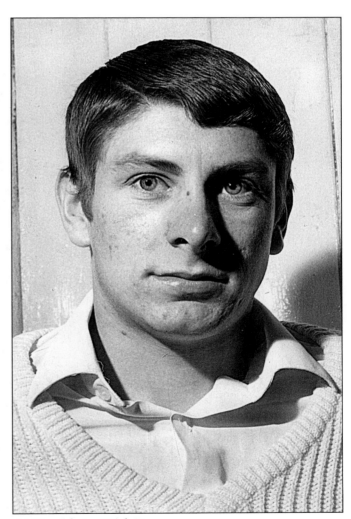

LMR cricketer Mick Burrows.

Cricketer John Austin.

Cricketer John Cotterell.

BOWLS

Members of the Park Road Bowling Club pictured at their annual dinner at the Royal Hotel on 28 January 1971.

Pictured after their bowls tournament on 19 September 1964 are (left to right) J. Stevens, who lost to J. Cooper, and W. Vawdrey, who lost to G. Slight.

Urban District Council chairman, Rowland Bowen, presenting the trophies at the Crewe, Nantwich and District Bowling Tournament at Park Road Bowling Club on 29 September 1962.

Liberal Club bowlers hamming it up for the camera on 20 April 1957.

Park Road Bowling Club veteran bowlers starting a game in the late 1960s.

Junior bowls winners pictured on 17 August 1967.

Bob Cross receiving the Cheshire County Merit Trophy on 19 July 1958.

Nantwich Liberal Club Bowlers pictured on 24 August 1963.

Park Road bowling team on 18 August 1966.

Bill Peake starting a bowling tournament on 21 September 1963.

Bernard Dutton (left) receives the President's Cup from Mr S. E. Ratcliffe, president of the South Cheshire Bowling League, after winning the Final at the Willaston Working Men's Club green on 4 September 1954.

Players who took part in the South Cheshire President's Bowling Handicap on 1 September 1956. Back row (left to right) are T. Hankey, C. Davenport, J. Steele (referee), C. Champion (runner-up) and G. Mattews. Front row: L. Cooper (winner), J. Lovatt, H. Wadkins and R. T. Case.

Nantwich UDC chairman Mr Joe Blagg presents a bowls tournament trophy on 24 September 1960.

Crewe players line up for a photograph on 4 May 1957.

Mr S. Chapman (left) receiving his trophy after winning the Willaston British Legion Trophy on 22 September 1955.

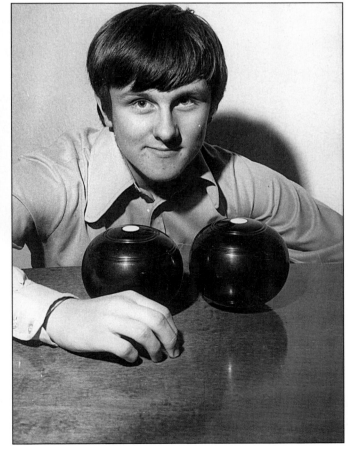

David Preston.

Dick Griffice, a winner in the 1960s.

Eddie Baskeyfield.

Dick Heaton in action in the Cheshire Merit Bowls Individual Cup. Looking on is his opponent, Chris Steele.

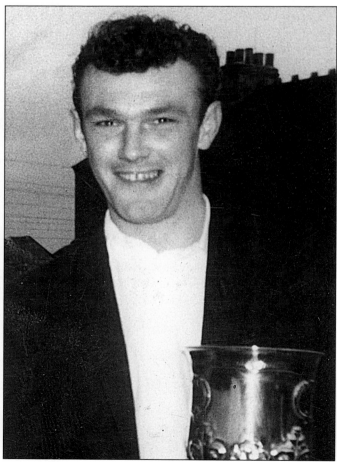

Club Union bowling winner Ron Heaton.

Fred Waddilove.

Dick Standring.

Glyn Vernon.

Peter Kelly.

Tom Hankey.

Lal Cooper with his trophy after winning the Club Union Bowls title in the 1960s.

Broad Street Workingmen's Club's successful bowling team pictured on 20 October 1968.

FISHING FOLK

Ken Bailey.

Paddy Doran.

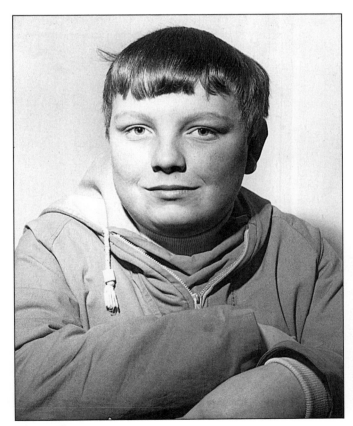

Linsay Capper.

Keith Major.

Dennis Lovell.

Brian 'Monty' Forster.

John Wright.

John Broomhall.

Dick Graham.

Stephen Edwards.

Mike Owens.

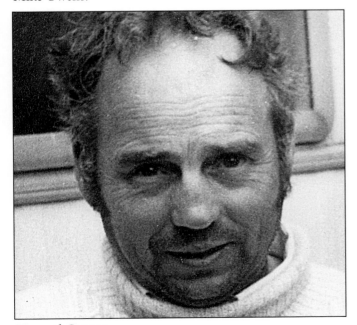

Howard Capper.

Dave Meakin.

Jeffrey Dolan.

Derek Wainwright.

Alan Wright.

David Holman.

Tony Lewis.

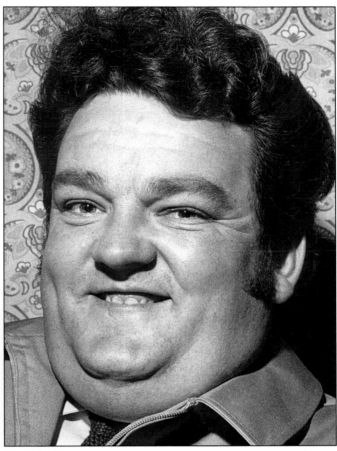

Fred Latham.

Tony Sheldon.

Gordon Penlington.

John Pimlott.

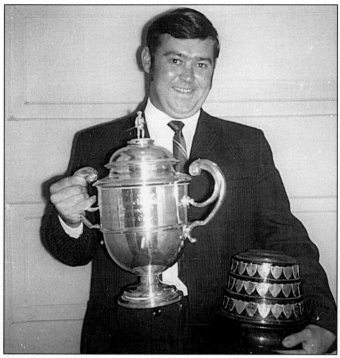

David Pace.

Amalgamated Anglers Club member, Bill Ollier, posing in front of his record 19¾lbs pike which beat the club's 42-year-old record.

Harry Birch.

Graham Massey.

David Capper.

Bill Houston.

Ray Jones.

Roy Goodier.

George Fisher.

Ron Summers.

Ernie Welch.

Trevor Howells.

Jack O'Hara.

Prize winners in a Valley Fishing Clubs match in the 1970s. The club went out of business some years ago.

Cyril Welch.

Roger Bampton.

Douglas Sturmey.

Ian Gilford.

Harry 'Hooky' Moulton.

Bill Edwards.

Terry Laycock.

FOOTBALL

Weston Football Club team, 1937.

Rankers FC, winners of a local knock-out competition when they beat Alton Villa in the late 1940s.

A football team from Crewe Grammar School – now Ruskin School – in 1942.

A 1947 Crewe Town Schoolboys team. Future Chelsea star Frank Blunstone is seated at the front, holding the ball.

A Crewe Villa football team from season 1948-49. Back row (left to right): J. Davies (secretary), J. Barker, Glyn Meredith, Bill Marks, Brian 'Monty' Forster, Middle row: G. Roberts, J. Barton, Roy 'Nipper' Walton, Bill Bowden, Ken Roberts. Front row: Billy Barker and John Bowyer.

Rolls-Royce departments played for the Morris Cup in 1951-52. This team represented the Fitting Bay. Back row (left to right) are George Brett, Ron Barker, Ray Mills, unknown, Al Gamage, Jack Edwards, Cliff Lindop, Les Gill, unknown, John Allcroft. Front row: Charlie Taylor, Jim Meachin, Jock Edmandson, Brian Ellson and Ken Wycherley.

County Clothes FC, Knock out Cup winners, 9 May 1964.

A Rolls-Royce Motors team which won the Commander Bayley Cup in the 1980s.

Hungerford Road School football team, winners of the Crewe and District Schools Shield in 1984.

Coppenhall FC team pictured outside the Cross Keys public house during the 1902-03 season. Joseph Palin is second from the right, back row.

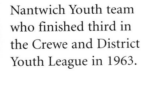

Nantwich Youth team who finished third in the Crewe and District Youth League in 1963.

An Alsager Town 'Lads and Dads' team.

Mill Street School football team, 1959.

Crewe and District Primary Schools football team in 1978-79 after winning the Tom Yeomen Shield.

Crewe and District Primary Schools football team, 1979-80.

Hightown Youth Club football team, 1958-59 season.

Willaston White Star football team, 1969-70.

Police Chief Inspector Ray Wilson, presenting a trophy to the tournament winners at Crewe Alexandra's all-weather pitch at the rear of the old Gresty Road stand in the 1980s.

Crewe Police Chief Superintendent Kenneth Newton with Manchester City chairman, the late Peter Swales, manager John Bond, players Joe Corrigan and Dennis Tueart, and Crewe police officers at a local M6 service station in 1981.

Referee Izaak Baker, the only Crewe man to take charge of an FA Cup Final at Wembley, was born in Shavington in 1873 and was employed at the Crewe North Locomotive Sheds in Station Street, where he made trimmings for steam engine oil lamps. After becoming a referee, his first appointment was to officiate a match at the Barony Field, Nantwich, where he received the grand sum of six old pence (less than 3p) for his services.

He went on to referee 22 international matches and take charge of the 1926 Bolton Wanderers v Manchester City Cup Final which ended in a 1-0 win for Bolton. Before the game he was presented to King George V. After hanging up his whistle he became a talent scout for Aston Villa and Liverpool.

He was life governor of the Crewe Memorial Hospital and helped raise numerous funds. He was honoured posthumously by Crewe and Nantwich Council in 1993 when his name was added to the local sporting roll of honour.

Local referee Keith Wright.

Ron Barker, who was appointed to the Football League linesmen's list in 1963-64 and promoted to the referees' list in 1967-68. He was one of Crewe's most active officials, once handling over 70 games in a season.

Local referee John Cotton.

Dave Wallace who was promoted the Football League list.

Local referee Peter Griffiths.

Local referee Phil Latham.

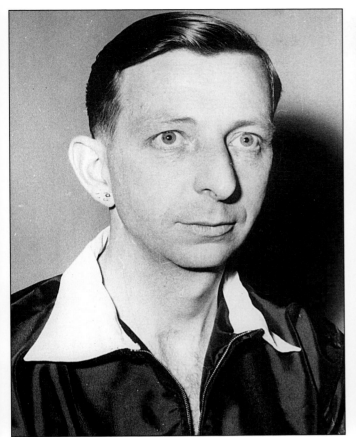

Cheshire FA referee Ken Hodgkinson.

Local referee John Preston.

Neville Ashley, another local referee who gained Football League status, is seen here with a team of local youngsters before a match on the Crewe Alexandra ground.

Local referee, the late Harry Vickers who was promoted to the football League list in the late 1960s.

Local referee Don Shaw.